5623 8503

COMMUNITY · CONNECTIONS
?

HOW DO THEY HELP?
THE SALVATION ARMY

BY KATIE MARSICO

CHERRY LAKE Publishing

Published in the United States of America by Cherry Lake Publishing
Ann Arbor, Michigan
www.cherrylakepublishing.com

Content Adviser: Cynthia Rathinasamy, Master of Public Policy, Concentration in
International Development, Gerald R. Ford School of Public Policy,
The University of Michigan, Ann Arbor, MI
Reading Adviser: Marla Conn, ReadAbility, Inc.

Photo Credits: ©jsmith/iStock, cover, 1; ©Brand X Pictures/Thinkstock, 5; ©Paul Sableman
/http://www.flickr.com/CC-BY-2.0, 7; ©Library of Congress/LC-DIG-ggbain-30603, 9;
©Library of Congress/LC-DIG-ggbain-10022, 11; ©JD Thomas/http://www.flickr.com/
CC-BY-SA 2.0, 13; ©Elvert Xavier Barnes Photography/http://www.flickr.com/CC-BY-2.0,
15; ©Howard Lake/http://www.flickr.com/CC-BY-SA 2.0, 17; ©Tyler Olson/
Shutterstock Images, 19; ©Jupiterimages/Thinkstock, 21

LIBRARY OF CONGRESS CATALOGING-IN-PUBLICATION DATA
Marsico, Katie, 1980-
 The Salvation Army / by Katie Marsico.
   pages cm. — (Community connections)
 Includes bibliographical references and index.
 ISBN 978-1-63188-029-2 (hardcover) — ISBN 978-1-63188-115-2 (pdf) —
ISBN 978-1-63188-072-8 (pbk.) — ISBN 978-1-63188-158-9 (ebook)
 1. Salvation Army–History–Juvenile literature. 2. Poor–Services for–Juvenile literature.
I. Title. BX9715.M37 2015
 287.9'6—dc23   2014006061

Cherry Lake Publishing would like to acknowledge the
work of The Partnership for 21st Century Skills. Please
visit www.p21.org for more information.

Printed in the United States of America
Corporate Graphics Inc.

THE SALVATION ARMY

CONTENTS

HOW DO THEY HELP?

MEANINGFUL MEALS

Hunger hurts and makes you tired. Yet having an empty stomach is part of life for many people. Some people don't always have money to buy food.

Fortunately, there are organized groups that feed people. The **Salvation** Army is one of them. It provides money to run soup kitchens. Soup kitchens offer hot meals, such as soup and

Soup kitchens are one way that the Salvation Army helps people.

THINK!

Think about how you'd feel if you had to go a few days without eating. Besides being hungry, what health problems would you face if you weren't able to eat regularly?

5

bread, to the needy, usually for free. Volunteers and workers make lunches and dinners every day.

The Salvation Army is a **charitable** religious organization. It is active in 126 nations, including the United States and Canada. It helps people living in **poverty**. It offers them food, clothes, shelter, and the chance to improve their lives. The Salvation Army also provides chances to learn about the Christian faith.

The red shield of the Salvation Army is found all over the world.

LOOK!

Go online with a parent, teacher, or other adult. Look for pictures of Salvation Army volunteers doing good in the United States and Canada. What services do you see being provided?

7

A PLAN TO SAVE THE POOR

A Christian **minister** named William Booth started the Salvation Army in London, England, in the 1860s. Booth hoped to spread religion among the poor. He created a place for the poor to worship. It was called the East London Christian **Mission**.

For many years, the Salvation Army has been giving food to those in need.

Who cared for the poor before the Salvation Army existed? Ask your teacher what life was like for people struggling with poverty in the 1800s. Find out who else offered help at that time.

By 1874, Booth had more than 1,000 volunteers and workers at his side. He thought of these men and women as spiritual soldiers. In 1878, Booth began calling his organization the Salvation Army.

The Salvation Army offered food and shelter to people living in poverty. It also helped some people to defeat alcohol **addiction** and to turn away from lives of crime.

The Salvation Army has collected holiday **donations** for many years.

THINK!

Members of the Salvation Army visited London's most dangerous areas. Sometimes they were even attacked! Why do you think Booth and his supporters continued to carry out their work?

11

Soon, other countries such as the United States and Canada started programs like the one in England. Over time, they began to offer a wider variety of social services.

The Salvation Army still tries to spread a message of hope through religion. Yet the organization does not deny anyone help simply because they don't share the same religious beliefs.

Thrift stores sell clothes, books, and furniture for very low prices. The money from sales helps groups such as the Salvation Army.

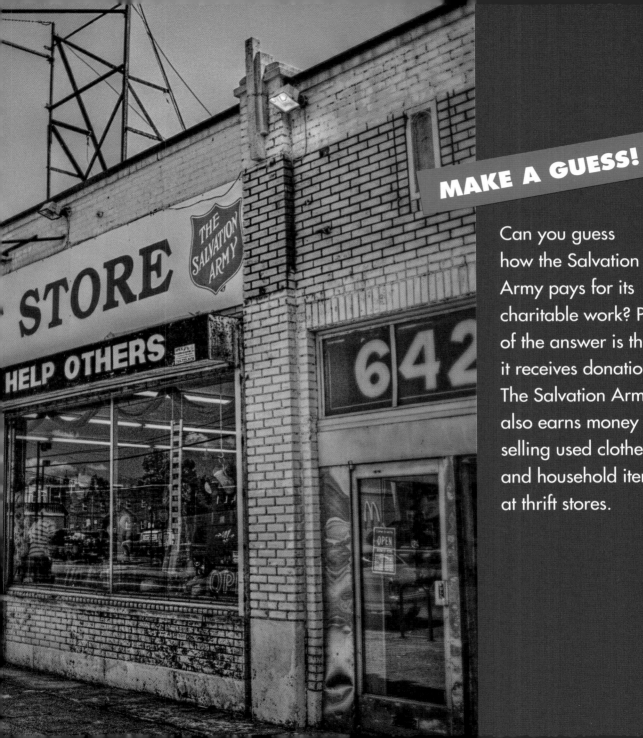

Can you guess how the Salvation Army pays for its charitable work? Part of the answer is that it receives donations. The Salvation Army also earns money by selling used clothes and household items at thrift stores.

13

The Salvation Army is not actually part of any national military group. Yet both are organized in similar ways. For example, certain workers in the Salvation Army wear uniforms and are known as officers and soldiers. This group depends on both volunteers and paid employees.

These volunteers are called bell ringers.

In November and December, look on street corners and at the entrance to local stores. Do you see anyone ringing a bell? Is the person standing next to a red kettle, or metal pot? People sometimes put money into these kettles. The Salvation Army uses this money to help others.

15

MORE THAN JUST FOOD

Today, the Salvation Army helps many people struggling with a wide range of challenges. It supplies the poor with meals at soup kitchens. Its food pantries give away everyday food items. The organization gives shelter to the homeless, as well. It offers job-training programs, too.

Drop boxes are one of many ways the Salvation Army collects donations.

OTHING
SHOES

SA070

ASK QUESTIONS!

Does the Salvation Army offer any services in your area? Ask your parents, teachers, and local leaders. Find out if these programs ever allow kids to volunteer!

17

The Salvation Army helps with more than poverty. It counsels people dealing with addiction, **domestic violence**, war, or natural disaster. The Salvation Army also works with prisoners and former criminals. It helps them rebuild their lives once they return to their communities.

The Salvation Army assists senior citizens, too. It offers

The Salvation Army helps educate children around the world.

Can you guess what services the Salvation Army offers kids? Make a few guesses, because this group runs many different youth programs! Some examples include summer and after-school camps, sporting events, and music and art activities.

classes, meal programs, and housing that help seniors stay active and healthy.

For some people, the Salvation Army means a hot meal or a roof over their head. For others, it means a chance to talk through their problems. Thanks to the Salvation Army, all these individuals are able to face the future with hope.

The Salvation Army helps improve the lives of people everywhere.

Create a "giving box" to keep in your kitchen. After a trip to the grocery store, try to place a new item inside. After the box is full, plan a family trip to a food pantry. Drop off your donations and start again!

GLOSSARY

addiction (uh-DIK-shuhn) a strong and dangerous need to regularly have something such as drugs or alcohol

charitable (CHER-uh-tuh-buhl) describes work that is done to help people in need

domestic violence (duh-MES-tik VYE-uh-luhns) violent or aggressive behavior between family members

donations (doh-NAY-shuhnz) money, food, clothes, or other items that are given to help someone in need

minister (MIH-nuh-stuhr) a person who serves as a spiritual leader within an organized religion

mission (MIH-shuhn) a building often used by a religious organization to offer charitable care or services

poverty (PAH-vuhr-tee) the state of being poor

salvation (sal-VAY-shuhn) the state of being saved or protected from sin, evil, or harm

FIND OUT MORE

BOOKS

Green, Robert. *Poverty*. Ann Arbor, MI: Cherry Lake Publishing, 2008.

Nelson, Maria. *I Can Volunteer*. New York: Gareth Stevens Publishing, 2014.

Senker, Cath. *Poverty and Hunger*. Mankato, MN: Smart Apple Media, 2012.

WEB SITES

Kids Can Make a Difference
www.kidscanmakeadifference.org
Check out this Web site to watch videos and read articles about how kids are tackling problems such as poverty and hunger.

The Salvation Army—Ways to Give
donate.salvationarmyusa.org or www.salvationarmy.ca
Visit these Web pages to learn about different opportunities for people of all ages to give to the Salvation Army.

INDEX

ABOUT THE AUTHOR

Katie Marsico is the author of more than 150 children's books. She lives in a suburb of Chicago, Illinois, with her husband and children.